The GOD WHO HATES LIES

Confronting & Rethinking Jewish Tradition

Study Guide

The Complete Study Companion to The God Who Hates Lies: Confronting & Rethinking Jewish Tradition by David Hartman with Charlie Buckholtz

CHARLIE BUCKHOLTZ

For People of All Faiths, All Backgrounds

JEWISH LIGHTS Publishing

The God Who Hates Lies: Confronting & Rethinking Jewish Tradition Study Guide

Published by Jewish Lights Publishing
www.jewishlights.com

CONTENTS

INTRODUCTION

In *The God Who Hates Lies: Confronting and Rethinking Jewish Tradition*, Rabbi David Hartman presents a compelling new take on what it means to be "religious" within the Jewish spiritual tradition. With a refreshing clarity of style and thought, he offers a new way of thinking about the intimate relationship between God and personal morality, and the role that these might play in the path of anyone seeking access to Jewish spirituality through the framework of halakha. This study guide will help you take some of the ideas and questions presented in *The God Who Hates Lies* and use them in classroom and learning settings. With you as their guide, this study guide will help you to help your students navigate a new understanding of, and relationship to, Jewish tradition.

1

HALAKHIC SPIRITUALITY
Living in the Presence of God

In this chapter, Rabbi Hartman explains the history of how halakha emerged as the central religious framework of Judaism. He offers his own concept of what halakha is, why he believes it is important, and how it has the potential to serve as a valuable spiritual resource for the contemporary Jewish community.

1) Why does Rabbi Hartman consider halakha to be central to Jewish life? (p. 27)

2) According to twentieth-century Judaism's great poet-theologian Abraham Joshua Heschel, what accounts for the widespread indifference to halakha among modern, enlightened Jews? What *doesn't* account for it? (p. 28)

3) How does the biblical image of God differ from that of the Talmud? What is the Talmud's new understanding of divine power? What changed to make this new conception of God possible and/or necessary? (pp. 32–36)

4) For the Talmudic Sages, what replaced history as the new medium within which to encounter the living reality of God? (p. 35)

5) How did the "Men of the Great Assembly" get their name? (p. 32)

6) What is the primary purpose of halakha, and how does it achieve that purpose? (pp. 37–40)

7) What is the essential distinction between Maimonides and Ravad in their debate about whether anthropomorphism should be considered heresy? What are their different understandings of what "God-consciousness" is and how it is achieved? (pp. 40–43)

8) Does halakhic spirituality emphasize the personal-existential ("This is *my* God and I will enshrine Him" [Exod. 15:2]) or the collective-historical ("…the God of *my father* and I will

exalt Him" [Exod. 15:2] religious quest? What elements of the tradition lead you to your answer? (pp. 43–47)

9) What do you think Rabbi Hartman means when he calls halakha not merely a legal structure but a "shared spiritual language" for the Jewish community? (p. 46)

2

TOWARD A
GOD-INTOXICATED HALAKHA

In this chapter, Rabbi Hartman elaborates upon the ways in which an emphasis on God-consciousness might influence the practice and evolution of halakha, individually and collectively. He explains the intimate relationship between God-consciousness and personal morality, and brings sources from within the tradition that seem to validate the expression of a personal, contingent moral voice even in the face of traditional authorities and precedents that reflect different moral sensibilities.

1) How does Rabbi Hartman's conception of halakha make room for the possibility of viewing halakha as an "open-ended educational system"? What does Rabbi Hartman mean by relating to halakha as an "educational experience"? (pp. 49–51)

2) In what ways might an emphasis upon God-consciousness in halakha impact its development? What are the questions this would force practitioners of halakha to ask? (p. 55)

3) How do you understand Buber's observation that "the imageless God has many images"? What are the implications of this statement for the development of halakha? (p. 55)

4) According to Maimonides, what type of knowledge does Moses ask God to reveal to him in the request, "Now, if I have truly gained Your favor, pray let me know Your ways"? (Exod. 33:13). (pp. 56–59)

5) What are the primary arguments used by religious "traditionalists" to challenge the validity of personal morality when it conflicts with the requirements of halakha? What type of religious personality does this attitude toward personal morality tend to cultivate? (pp. 60–63)

6) Are there any strains within Jewish tradition that seem to legitimize the expression of a personal moral voice? (p. 63)

7) According to the Talmud, who is the group referred to in the verse about the "tears of the oppressed"? (Eccles. 4:1). Who is oppressing them, and how? (pp. 63–64)

8) What approaches do the Talmudic Rabbis take toward the morally problematic case of the "rebellious son"? What different ethical sensibilities are reflected in their responses? (pp. 66–68)

9) How does Rabbi Hartman interpret the opinion of Rabbi Yonatan at the end of the "rebellious son" discussion: "I saw a 'stubborn and rebellious son,' and I sat on his grave"? (BT *Sanhedrin* 72a). (p. 68)

3

FEMINISM AND APOLOGETICS
Lying in the Presence of God

In this chapter, Rabbi Hartman examines and critiques the ways in which prominent modern Orthodox theologians have responded to the moral challenge of feminism. He shows that the dominant approach has consisted of "apologetics"—theological contortions that attempt to claim that Jewish tradition actually upholds the value of equality between men and women. Rabbi Hartman introduces sources that illustrate the ways in which the subservience of women to men, particularly in the marital relationship, have been promoted as positive moral values expressing ultimate divine wisdom and benevolence. He discusses the image of God that supports this approving view of gender imbalance, and the ways in which appropriating a different image of God might lead to a transformation of gender relationships within the halakhic framework.

1) What is the "*aguna* problem" and how is it a challenge to the moral credibility of halakha? How have those in the contemporary halakhic community responded to this problem? How have these responses to the *aguna* problem mirrored those of the Talmudic Sages to the law of the "rebellious son"? What image of God seems to lie behind their approach? (pp. 69–72)

2) In his book *Family Redeemed*, how does Rabbi Joseph B. Soloveitchik respond to the claim that Jewish tradition promotes gender inequality? How does he define the nature of male and female roles within the marriage relationship? What are the features of this response that lead Rabbi Hartman to characterize it as "apologetic"? (pp. 73–76)

3) In the Talmudic story about Rabban Gamliel's daughter, what does she claim is the reason for the creation of woman, and what image does she invoke to illustrate this reason? (pp. 76–77) Why, according to the Talmud, is it more difficult for a (married) woman to fulfill the commandment to "revere one's father and mother" than a man? (pp. 77–78) How is the dominant Talmudic imagery and attitude toward woman as a "helper" to man reflected in the laws of marriage and divorce? (pp. 78–82)

4) What does Eliezer Berkowitz mean by his distinction between laws that are "Torah-tolerated" versus those that are "Torah-directed" or "Torah-taught"? What conceptual solution does he propose to the seemingly contradictory attitudes of Maimonides toward the treatment and status of wives in the marital relationship? (pp. 84–87) Why does Rabbi Hartman consider even Berkowitz's approach to be "apologetic"? What alternative solution does he propose to the contradiction found in Maimonides? (pp. 88–89)

5) According to the Talmud, how do women fulfill the commandment of Torah study? (p. 89) Why are they exempt from a "strict" application of this commandment? What impact does their formal exemption from Torah study have upon their status within the ritual life of the community? (pp. 89–91) What reason does Rabbi Samson Raphael Hirsch, a founding figure of modern Orthodoxy in nineteenth-century Germany, give for women's exemption from positive, time-bound mitzvot? (p. 92)

6) How does Rabbi Aaron Soloveitchik respond to the feminist critique of halakha that was embraced by liberal non-Orthodox movements within Judaism? What Jewish texts and theological concepts does he use to justify his argument? How does he explain women's exemption from positive, time-bound mitzvot? (pp. 93–97)

7) How do Hirsch, A. Soloveitchik, and Rabbi Yaakov ben Asher, respectively, interpret the blessing, "… who created me according to His will," prescribed by halakha to women upon awakening in the morning? (pp. 96–100)

8) What are some of the sources within the tradition that reflect halakha's attitude toward the role of women in public life? What rationale is presented for this stance? (pp. 102–104)

9) According to Rabbi Hartman, why, ultimately, has the halakhic issue of *aguna* not yet been solved? (pp. 104–106) What image of God is reflected in the modern, liberal spirit of egalitarianism? (p. 106) How might this image of God be appropriated within individual halakhic life and communal halakhic development? (pp. 106–109)

4

BIOLOGY OR COVENANT?
Conversion and the Corrupting Influence of Gentile Seed

In this chapter, Rabbi Hartman discusses different views within the tradition as to the identity status of the convert, the nature of conversion itself, and the image of God that supports and fuels these alternate views. He shows how using a "hermeneutic of God-consciousness" might help to guide which of these views we choose to emphasize in our individual and communal halakhic lives.

1) What is the reason given by Jewish tradition for preventing *kohanim* (priests) from marrying female converts? What larger questions does this stance raise about the tradition's attitude toward the status of converts generally? What unresolved conceptual tension within the tradition do these questions reveal? (pp. 113–114)

2) How do statements like that of Maimonides—"A convert, upon conversion, is like a newborn baby"—seem to present a challenge or contradiction to the law against *kohanim* marrying converts? (p. 114) What other sources from within the tradition seem to support this way of thinking about conversion and converts? How does the case of the bastard–Torah-scholar vs. the *kohen*–ignoramus factor into this discussion? (pp. 114–116) What image of God underlies this strain of Rabbinic thought? (p. 116)

3) What is the question Maimonides received from Ovadiah? What deeper theological question does Maimonides take Ovadiah's query as an opportunity to address? (pp. 116–117; p. 122)

4) What are some sources within Jewish tradition that support the notion that a "complete" Jewish identity can only be achieved through a biological connection to Jewish familial history? (pp. 117–120)

5) What is meant by the term "holy seed," and why did Ezra begin to use it as the dominant criterion of Jewish identity? (pp. 120–121) How did the understanding and process of conversion shift in the Rabbinic period? What conception of the convert's status is reflected in

the Talmudic term, "brother in mitzvot"? (p. 121) What conception of the convert's status has been favored by kabbalists like Rabbi Yehuda Halevi? (pp. 121–122)

6) How does Maimonides answer Ovadiah's question? (pp. 122–125) For Maimonides, what is the constitutive principle of Jewish identity and the only meaningful standard by which a person becomes a "disciple of Abraham"? (p. 123) How does Maimonides seem to interpret the Talmudic statement, "because Abraham was the father of the entire world"? (PT Bikkurim 1:4) (pp. 124–125). What image of God does Maimonides' response to Ovadiah invoke? (p. 125)

7) What legal rulings of Maimonides seem to contradict the position he articulates in his response to Ovadiah? (pp. 125–126) How might we understand this contradiction, and what questions does it raise? (p. 127) For what purpose does the Talmud use the phrase "not from among *the choice ones* among your brothers"? (BT *Bava Kama* 88a). (p. 126)

8) How does Maimonides's response to Ovadiah employ what Rabbi Hartman calls a "hermeneutic of God-consciousness"? (p. 128)

9) How would you explain the theological basis of Rabbi Hartman's decision to marry Peter and Susan, despite Peter being a *kohen* and Susan being a convert? (pp. 128–130)

5

WHERE DID MODERN ORTHODOXY GO WRONG?

The Mistaken Halakhic Presumptions of Rabbi Soloveitchik

In this chapter, Rabbi Hartman addresses the question of why halakha in the modern period has been so resistant to critique and change. He examines the theological basis of this fear of change through the lens of Rabbi Joseph B. Soleveitchik, whose "meta-halakhic" thinking has served as a lynchpin—one might even say an article of faith—of modern Orthodox theology. He also presents an alternative view of halakhic change through the lens of another significant modern Orthodox thinker, Rabbi Emanuel Rackman, who believed that progress, not stasis, is a hallmark of halakhic authenticity. He discusses the different images of God that underpin and animate these opposing views.

1) How would Rabbi Soloveitchik have judged Rabbi Hartman's decision to marry Peter and Susan? How do we know this? What was the basis of Rabbi Soloveitchik's decision? (pp. 131–132)

2) What is meant by the "meta-halakhic" sphere? What are some examples of meta-halakhic questions? What role do such questions play in the evolution of halakha? What is their relationship to "the anti-change theology that has guided so much of modern halakhic development"? (p. 133)

3) What does Rabbi Hartman mean by the "theology of halakhic perfection"? What type of perfection is being referred to here, and what are its implications for halakha? What must be surrendered or sacrificed in order for this perfection to be achieved? (pp. 134–135)

4) According to Rabbi Emanuel Rackman, why had the *aguna* issue not been solved in his time? (p. 138) How did his stance on meta-halakhic questions lead him to this conclusion? (pp. 135–138)

5) What is meant by the Talmudic term *hazaka*, or "presumption"? What is the role of *hazaka* in legal decision-making? (p. 139) What particular Talmudic *hazaka* is under discussion in Rabbi Rackman's *aguna* proposal? (pp. 140–143) What position did Rabbi Rackman take toward this *hazaka* and toward *hazakot* in general? (p. 143) How did this position lead to his proposed solution to the *aguna* problem?

6) Why are Jewish communities living outside Israel bound by halakha to observe an "extra" day of the major Jewish festivals? Why does Rabbi Hartman use this as an example of "the strong Talmudic tendency to view received tradition as a value unto itself"? (pp. 145–146)

7) According to Soloveitchik's "credo," what must be surrendered or sacrificed in order to access the power of authentic Torah study? What does he claim is gained through this sacrifice? Why do "secular systems of values" pose a threat to authentic Torah study? (pp. 147–148)

8) What is Soloveitchik's stance on the nature and significance of *hazakot*? How does it differ from Rackman's? (p. 149) How does Soloveitchik understand, in particular, the *hazaka* at issue in Rackman's *aguna* proposal? (pp. 148–150) What did he consider to be the consequence of implementing Rackman's proposal? What view of women does Soloveitchik insist upon maintaining? (pp. 150–151) Why does Rabbi Hartman characterize Soloveitchik as implementing an "infallibility principle" and what does he mean by this term? (p. 151)

9) According to Rabbi Hartman, what are the dangers posed by Rabbi Soloveitchik's perception of halakha—why does he consider it to be "devastating to halakhic culture"? (pp. 153–154) What alternative vision of "halakhic spirituality" does Hartman offer in its place? (pp. 154–155) What does he propose as being the "benefit" of Soloveitchik's approach? (p. 155) In the midrash about the Men of the Great Assembly restoring an original prayer formulation that had for a time been altered by the prophets Jeremiah and Daniel, what does it mean that they "did not want to ascribe false things to God"? What are the "false things" they were committed to avoiding? (pp. 155–156)

6

THE GOD WHO HATES LIES
Choosing Life in the Midst of Uncertainty

In this chapter, Rabbi Hartman discusses the challenges and opportunities posed by the emergence of the State of Israel for the inherited halakhic system. He presents his own view of the religious significance of history, developing a "theology of response" through which our responses to historical developments are incorporated into the halakhic life of the community. He explains his understanding of the core religious meaning of the State of Israel, as well as Jewish self-identification in a post-Shoah world, and elaborates ways in which these profound covenantal statements might be given weight within the halakhic system, particularly with respect to the issue of conversion.

1) What challenges and questions does the emergence of the State of Israel pose to the inherited halakhic system? (p. 159) What aspect of this challenge is highlighted by the Tisha B'Av prayer? (pp. 159–161)

2) Why does Rabbi Hartman cite the story of the Israeli soldier who was denied full Jewish burial as "an instance in which the halakhic system had failed to formulate a constructive response to the complex, emerging social realities of Jewish life in Israel"? (pp. 161–163)

3) Who is the person described by Maimonides as the *poresh mi-darkei tzibur*, or, "one who separates oneself from the ways of the community"—that is, what is the nature and expression of this sin? (p. 164) What community does Rabbi Hartman argue represents a contemporary example of this category, and why? What examples does he offer to support this claim? (pp. 163–166)

4) According to Rabbi Hartman, what is the central question around which the complicated secular-religious debate in Israel ultimately revolves? (p. 165) What is meant by the term *tzibur*? (p. 165) What is the true importance of the "Who is a Jew" question? (p. 165)

5) What are the implications of the question, "Is Israel an authentic community for mediating the Jewish story?" Practically, how does the development of society and halakha differ based on how we answer this question? (p. 166) What type of answer to this question emerges, according to Rabbi Hartman, if we allow ourselves to be guided by "the God who hates lies"? (pp. 166–167)

6) What, according to Rabbi Hartman, is the "core meaning" of the State of Israel? (p. 167) Why does Rabbi Hartman assign special religious status to Israeli soldiers? (p. 167) What is the basis of his suggestion that the Israeli soldier, who was denied a full Jewish burial, "should have been granted full status as a Jew"? (p. 168) What roles might the concept of *dam brit* (blood of the covenant) and the example of the biblical Ruth play in formulating what he calls "a creative response to issues of Jewish identity status"? (pp. 168–169)

7) What does Rabbi Hartman mean when he suggests that certain contemporary Orthodox communities have an "authority fetish"? How does this focus on authority contradict what he sees as the central value of the State of Israel? How does the trend of retroactive conversions reflect an example of this misguided focus? What are other examples? (pp. 170–172)

8) "The emergence of a self-confident American Jewry after the Shoah is itself a religious act; to identify with the Jewish people is not just a national, but a *covenantal* statement." How does Rabbi Hartman feel this covenantal statement should affect Jewish conversion policy? (pp. 173–174) What would be the implications of viewing conversion as a "leap into the possible"? (p. 174) How might this view shape our understanding of "receiving the mitzvot" as a requirement for conversion? What are some sources within the tradition that might support this understanding? (pp. 174–175) How is it supported by the "living Jewish society" of Israel? (p. 175) How is its spirit reflected in the Law of Return? (pp. 175–176)

9) What does Rabbi Hartman mean by a "theology of response"? What understanding of history underlies this theology? (pp. 176–177) What about the emergence of the State of Israel makes it worthy of such a response? (pp. 178–180) What is the meaning of Martin Buber's assertion that the kibbutz was "an experiment that did not fail," and why does Rabbi Hartman agree with him? (pp. 180–181)

Printed in the USA
CPSIA information can be obtained
at www.ICGtesting.com
JSHW060050150824
68134JS00031B/2701